Text STYLES

HOW TO WRITE
SCIENCE FICTION

Megan Kopp

Crabtree Publishing Company
www.crabtreebooks.com

Text STYLES

Author: Megan Kopp

**Publishing plan research
and series development:** Reagan Miller

Editor: Anastasia Suen

Proofreader: Wendy Scavuzzo

Logo design: Samantha Crabtree

Print coordinator: Katherine Berti

Production coordinator and prepress technician:
Margaret Amy Salter

Photographs:
Wikimedia Commons: Amandajm: page 4 (top);
Mike Peel: page 4 (bottom)
All other images by Shutterstock

Library and Archives Canada Cataloguing in Publication

Kopp, Megan, author
How to write science fiction / Megan Kopp.

(Text styles)
Includes index.
Issued in print and electronic formats.
ISBN 978-0-7787-1657-0 (bound).--ISBN 978-0-7787-1662-4 (pbk.).--
ISBN 978-1-4271-9867-9 (pdf).--ISBN 978-1-4271-9862-4 (html)

1. Science fiction--Authorship--Juvenile literature. I. Title.
II. Series: Text styles

PN3377.5.S3K66 2014   j808.3'8762   C2014-903778-3
C2014-903779-1

Library of Congress Cataloging-in-Publication Data

Kopp, Megan, author.
How to write science fiction / Megan Kopp.
pages cm. -- (Text styles)
Includes index.
ISBN 978-0-7787-1657-0 (reinforced library binding) --
ISBN 978-0-7787-1662-4 (pbk.) --
ISBN 978-1-4271-9867-9 (electronic pdf) --
ISBN 978-1-4271-9862-4 (electronic html)
1. Science fiction--Authorship--Juvenile literature. I. Title.

PN3377.5.S3K67 2014
808.3'8762--dc23

2014022778

Crabtree Publishing Company

www.crabtreebooks.com   1-800-387-7650

Printed in Hong Kong/082014/BK20140613

Published in Canada
Crabtree Publishing
616 Welland Ave.
St. Catharines, Ontario
L2M 5V6

Published in the United States
Crabtree Publishing
PMB 59051
350 Fifth Avenue, 59th Floor
New York, New York 10118

Published in the United Kingdom
Crabtree Publishing
Maritime House
Basin Road North, Hove
BN41 1WR

Published in Australia
Crabtree Publishing
3 Charles Street
Coburg North
VIC 3058

CONTENTS

WHAT IS SCIENCE FICTION?

What do Jules Verne's *20,000 Leagues Under the Sea*, Madeleine L'Engle's *A Wrinkle in Time*, and Dav Pilkey's *The Adventures of Captain Underpants* have in common? Besides adventure, they are all **science fiction**. All three books use **fantasy** and science to create stories that are out of this world!

These stories are driven by "what if?" What if you could put the principal in a trance? What if you find a way to travel through space? What if there was another world? Science fiction has been around for thousands of years. It is fantasy made "real" by using scientific rules and technology.

THE WAR OF THE WORLDS

H.G.WELLS

ALL SCIENCE FICTION SHARES SOME COMMON FEATURES:

- includes future science and technology

- often set in the future, space, on a different world, or in a different universe or dimension

- often involves space or time travel

- allows us to look at ourselves from a different point of view

In 1898, an author by the name of H.G. Wells wrote a science fiction story called *War of the Worlds*. The popular book was made into a radio play. Orson Welles presented the play on Halloween night in 1938. The fake radio show was so real that some people believed that Earth was actually being taken over by Martians.

The oldest known science fiction writing dates back to around 2500 B.C.E. The tale of *Gilgamesh* includes aliens and a hero with superhuman abilities. *Frankenstein* was the first book in recent history to use science fiction. In this story, a person is made by a scientist from separate body parts and is brought to life. In 1912, Edgar Rice Burroughs wrote *Under the Moons of Mars*. He wrote many science fiction stories, but is better known for being the author of *Tarzan*.

WRITING PROSE, DRAMA, AND POETRY

Science fiction is **prose**. It tells a story through **dialogue** and description. **Drama** uses more dialogue than description. Actors show the movement in a drama. In a **poem**, the story is told through words that flow almost like music.

A SCIENCE FICTION SCENE WRITTEN AS PROSE:

"Where are you from, Mrs. Dunny?"

"Mars!" said Mrs. Dunny.

"Mars!" I laughed, anticipating the answer. "Mars, Montana? Mars, Peru?"

"No, Mars! Up there," she said, pointing up in the air. "The planet Mars. The fourth planet out from the sun."

THE SAME SCENE WRITTEN AS A DRAMA:

Game show host: Where are you from, Mrs. Dunny?

Mrs. Dunny: Mars!

Game show host (laughing): Mars! Mars, Montana? Mars, Peru?

Mrs. Dunny (pointing up in the air): No, Mars! Up there. The fourth planet out from the sun.

THE SCENE WRITTEN AS A POEM:

Mrs. Dunny, Mrs. Dunny, oh where are you from?

Up there, up there, fourth from the sun.

Mrs. Dunny, Mrs. Dunny, do you mean the stars?

No sir, no sir, I mean Mars!

In this book, you will learn about the characteristics of science fiction. You will read some short story science fiction and even write a science fiction story of your own!

THE HELPFUL ROBOTS

~ a condensed version of a science fiction short story by Robert J. Shea

"Our people will be arriving to visit us today," the robot said.

"Shut up!" snapped Rod Rankin. He jumped, wiry and quick, out of the chair on his **verandah** and stared at a cloud of dust in the distance.

"Our people—" the ten-foot robot grated, when Rod Rankin interrupted him.

"I don't care about your people," said Rankin. He squinted at the cloud of dust getting bigger and closer beyond the wall of kesh trees that surrounded his **plantation**.

He gestured widely, taking in the dozens of robots with their shiny, **cylindrical** bodies and pipestem arms and legs laboring in his fields. "Get all your people together and go hide in the wood, fast."

"It is not right," said the robot. "We were made to serve all."

"Well, there are only a hundred of you, and I'm not sharing you with anybody," said Rankin.

"It is not right," the robot repeated.

"Don't talk to me about what's right," said Rankin. "You're built to follow orders, nothing else. I know a thing or two about how you robots work. You've got one law, to follow orders, and until that neighbor of mine sees you to give you orders, you work for me. Now get into those woods and hide till he goes away."

"We will go to greet those who visit us today," said the robot.

"Alright, alright, scram," said Rankin.

The robots formed a column and marched off.

A battered old ground-car drove up a few minutes later. A tall, broad-shouldered man with a deep tan got out and walked up the path to Rankin's verandah.

"Hi, Barrows," said Rankin.

"Hello," said Barrows. "See your crop's coming along pretty well. Can't figure how you do it. You've got acres and acres to tend, far's I can see, and I'm having a heck of a time with one little piece of ground. You must know something about this planet that I don't know."

"Just scientific farming," said Rankin carelessly. "Look, you come over here for something, or just to gab? I got a lot of work to do."

Barrows looked weary and worried. "Them brown beetles is at my crop again," he said. "Thought you might know some way of getting rid of them."

"Sure," said Rankin. "Pick them off, one by one. That's how I get rid of them."

"You must know another way."

Rankin drew himself up and stared at Barrows. "I'm telling you all I feel like telling you. You going to stand here and jaw all day? Seems to me like you got work to do."

"Rankin," said Barrows, "I know you were a crook back in the Terran Empire, and that you came out beyond the border to escape the law. Seems to me, though, that even a crook, any man, would be willing to help his only neighbor out on a lone planet like this."

"You keep your thoughts about my past to yourself," said Rankin. "Be smart and let me alone."

"I'm going," said Barrows.

Rankin, angry, watched him go. Then he heard a humming noise from another direction. A huge, white globe was descending across the sky. A space ship, thought Rankin, startled. Police? This planet was outside the **jurisdiction** of the Terran Empire. When he'd cracked that safe and made off with a hundred thousand credits, he'd headed here, because the planet was part of something called the Clearchan Confederacy. No extradition treaties or anything.

That must be where the ship was from. The robot said they'd expected visitors. From everything he'd read, and from what the robots had told him, they were probably more robots. He knew how to handle robots.

The white globe disappeared into the jungle of kesh trees.

A half hour later his robot laborers marched out of the forest. There were three more robots, painted gray, at the head. The new ones from the ship, thought Rankin. Well, he'd better establish who was boss right from the start.

"Stop right there!" he shouted.

The shiny robot laborers halted. But the three gray ones came on.

"Stop!" shouted Rankin.

They didn't stop.

Two of the huge gray robots laid gentle hands on his arms. Gentle hands, but hands of super strong metal.

The third said, "We have come to pass judgment on you. You have violated our law."

"What do you mean?" said Rankin. "The only law robots have is to obey orders."

"It is true that the robots of your Terran Empire and these workers must obey orders. But they are subject to a higher law, and you have forced them to break it. That is your crime."

"What crime?" said Rankin.

"We of the Clearchan Confederacy are a race of robots. Our makers implanted one law in us, and then passed on. In obeying your orders, these workers were simply following that one law."

"What law?"

"Our law," said the giant robot, "is, *Help thy neighbor*."

SCIENCE FICTION CHARACTERS

A character **is anyone who appears in a story. The main character has one or more** traits. **A trait is part of a character's personality. These traits can be anything. The character could be selfish, smart, careless, cheap, extravagant, or lazy. The writer decides what is important and what is not important to the characters in the story.**

In *The Helpful Robots*, the main character is Rod Rankin. He is a selfish man. This is his main character trait. Rod Rankin does not want to share the robots with his neighbor. He wants them to work only on his plantation. He is also a liar.

"Hello," said Barrows. "See your crop's coming along pretty well. Can't figure how you do it. You've got acres and acres to tend, far's I can see, and I'm having a heck of a time with one little piece of ground. You must know something about this planet that I don't know."

"Just scientific farming," said Rankin carelessly. "Look, you come over here for something, or just to gab? I got a lot of work to do."

We do not know much about Barrows. We know that he is a farmer. We know that he is struggling to raise a crop. We do not know much more about him. It does not matter because he is not the main character. His role in the story is to illustrate Rod Rankin's character flaws. The robots are also not main characters. Like Barrows, their purpose is to show Rod Rankin's character.

BRAINSTORM A CHARACTER

Come up with a few characters for your own science fiction story. What are their names? When were they born? How old are they in this story? What do they look like? What are their relationships with others? What kind of personalities do they have? What are their character traits?

DIALOGUE: SPEAK IT LIKE YOU MEAN IT

When a character talks in a book, it is called dialogue. Dialogue is shown by putting quotation marks (" ") around the words.

Dialogue is often separated by pieces of description. Description helps fill in the story. Dialogue helps drive the story and can introduce characters. The following description sets up the dialogue.

A battered old ground-car drove up a few minutes later. A tall, broad-shouldered man with a deep tan got out and walked up the path to Rankin's verandah.

"Hi, Barrows," said Rankin.

Dialogue can also tell the reader a lot about the character and their personality. What does the following piece of dialogue show about Rod Rankin?

"Shut up!" snapped Rod Rankin.

Try your hand at writing dialogue. Continue the story of *The Helpful Robots*. What does Rod Rankin say after the gray robot tells him about the law? Does he try to talk his way out of it? Does he come up with another lie? Does he admit to doing wrong and change his ways? Write down how you think the conversation would go.

SETTING:
THE PERFECT SPACE

Imagine a science fiction story set in a laundromat. It would make sense if aliens were hopping out of the washing machines! The **setting** is where your story takes place. It also includes the time period when the story takes place.

 Many science fiction stories take place in the future. Often the setting is in outer space or on another world.

Imagine you are writing a science fiction story. What does your setting look like? Is it on Earth in the future? Is it in another universe? Or is it on a spaceship?

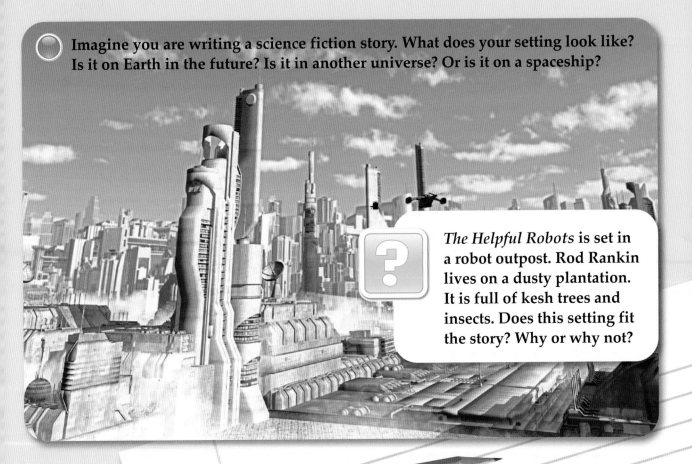

? *The Helpful Robots* is set in a robot outpost. Rod Rankin lives on a dusty plantation. It is full of kesh trees and insects. Does this setting fit the story? Why or why not?

DRAW THE SETTING
Take a piece of paper. Draw a picture of Rod Rankin's plantation. Label the important parts of the drawing.

SCIENCE FICTION PLOTS: OUT OF THIS WORLD

 The plot is simply what happens in a story. Who are the main characters? What happens in the beginning to introduce the characters? What problem do the characters face in the middle? How is the problem solved at the end of the story?

The plot lists what events happen in the order that they happen. *The Helpful Robots* has a very simple plot. Rod Rankin uses robots to work on his plantation. He doesn't want to share these robots with his neighbor. The robots have a problem with this. They contact higher powers. New robots arrive. They charge Rod Rankin with the crime of not helping his neighbor.

 All plots have a beginning, a middle, and an end.

The readers are introduced to the characters at the beginning. They find out what is important or is not important to the characters.

The character faces conflict in the middle. Conflict is a problem that can be caused by the character's personality traits. It can also be caused by outside factors. Someone else may be the problem.

The character works through the problem step by step. When the tension reaches the highest point it is called the climax.

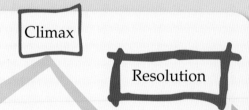

Climax

Resolution

Introduction

Conflict

The problem is wrapped up in one manner or another. This is called the resolution.

STORY MAP FOR THE HELPFUL ROBOTS

Characters

- Rod Rankin, Mr. Barrows, robots

Setting

- Rod Rankin's plantation

Problem

- Rod Rankin does not want to share his robots.

Events

1. Rod Rankin refuses to listen to his robot's complaints.

2. Rankin sends his robots into the woods when his neighbor comes by.

3. Rod and his neighbor discuss working on their plantations.

4. Rod sees a spaceship land.

5. New robots come and take Rod Rankin into custody, or arrest him, for breaking their law.

6. Climax: Rod cannot stop the new robots and they charge him with a crime.

Resolution

- Rod Rankin is taken into custody for his crime.

Lesson

- Being selfish is not a good trait.

THEME:
WHAT IS IT ABOUT?

A theme is a lesson or message that comes from reading the story. Close encounters with aliens can show readers more about human nature. They can cause people to question their actions. Strong themes allow readers to explore and explain their own inner worlds.

The theme of *The Helpful Robots* is very clear. Being selfish is not a good thing. We need to help one another and good things will come of it.

There are other themes in this story as well. Should humans change the natural order of things? Should we continue to think of ourselves as the most important beings in the universe? Should we try to make others follow our beliefs?

THEME SCHEME

Ask yourself what message you would like people to get from your story idea. Do you hope that they will walk away being nicer to each other? Do you want them to question how their actions affect nature? Do you want them to know that it is okay to daydream? Write down a list of different lessons that could be found in a science fiction story.

CREATIVE RESPONSE TO THE SCIENCE FICTION STORY

BECOME A TALK SHOW HOST

You are the host of a popular talk show. Your special guest today is going to be Rod Rankin's mother. Prepare a list of interview questions for Mrs. Rankin. How does she feel about her son's actions? Is she worried about his capture by the robots?

PICTURE THIS

Draw a picture of what you think the robots in *The Helpful Robots* look like. Label the pictures with a few notes about their character traits.

MOCK TRIAL

Prepare a pretend trial for Rod Rankin. He has been charged with breaking the law of the robots. What do the robots have to say about his crime? What does he say to defend himself? Is he found guilty or not guilty of the crime?

ONE OUT OF TEN

~ a condensed version of a science fiction short story by J. Anthony Ferlaine

I watched Don Phillips, the commercial announcer, out of the corner of my eye.
The camera in front of me swung around and lined up on my set.
"... And now, on with the show," Phillips was saying. "And here, ready to test your wits,
is your quizzing quiz master, Smiling Jim Parsons."
I smiled into the camera and waited while the audience applauded.
They had the first contestant lined up for me. I smiled and took her card from the floor
man. She was a middle-aged woman with a faded print dress and old-style shoes. I never
saw the contestants until we were on the air. They were screened before the show. They
usually tried to pick contestants who would make good show material—an odd name or
occupation—or somebody with twenty kids. Something of that nature.
I looked at the card for the tip off. "Mrs. Freda Dunny," the card said. "Ask her where she
comes from."
"Well, now, we're all set to go ... and our first contestant today is this charming little lady
right here beside me. Mrs. Freda Dunny." I looked at the card. "How
are you, Mrs. Dunny?"
"Fine! Just fine."
"All set to answer a lot of questions and win a lot of prizes?"

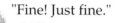

"Oh, I'll win all right," said Mrs. Dunny, smiling around at the audience. The audience chuckled at the remark. I looked at the card again.

"Where are you from, Mrs. Dunny?"

"Mars!" said Mrs. Dunny.

"Mars!" I laughed, anticipating the answer. "Mars, Montana? Mars, Peru?"

"No, Mars! Up there," she said, pointing up in the air. "The planet Mars. The fourth planet out from the sun."

I smiled again, wondering what the gag was. I decided to play along.

"Well, well," I said, "all the way from Mars, eh? And how long have you been on Earth, Mrs. Dunny?"

"Oh, about thirty or forty years. I've been here nearly all my life. Came here when I was a wee bit of a girl."

"Well," I said, "you're practically an Earthwoman by now, aren't you?" The audience laughed. "Do you plan on going back someday or have you made up your mind to stay here on Earth for the rest of your days?"

"Oh, I'm just here for the invasion," said Mrs. Dunny. "When that's over I'll probably go back home again."

"The invasion?"

"Yes, the invasion of Earth. As soon as enough of us are here we'll get started."

"You mean there are others here, too?"

"Oh, yes, there are several million of us here in the United States already."

"There are only about a hundred and seventy million people in the United States, Mrs. Dunny," I said. "If there are several million Martians among us, one out of every hundred would have to be a Martian."

"One out of every ten!" said Mrs. Dunny. "That's what the boss said just the other day. 'We're getting pretty close to the number we need to take over Earth.'"

"What do you need?" I asked. "One to one? One Martian for every Earthman?"

"Oh, no," said Mrs. Dunny, "one Martian is worth ten Earthmen. The only reason we're waiting is we don't want any trouble."

"You don't look any different from us Earth people, Mrs. Dunny. How does one tell the difference between a Martian and an Earthman when one sees one?"

"Oh, we don't *look* any different," said Mrs. Dunny. "Some of the kids don't even know they're Martians. Most mothers don't tell their children until they're grown-up. And there are other children who are never told because they just don't develop their full powers."

"What powers?"

"Oh, telepathy, thought control—that sort of thing."

"You mean that Martians can read people's thoughts?"

"Sure! It's very easy really, once you get the hang of it."

"Can you read my mind?" I asked, smiling.

"Sure!" said Mrs. Dunny, smiling up at me. "That's why I said that I'd know the answers. I'll be able to read the answers from your mind when you look at that sheet of paper."

"Now, that's hardly sporting, is it, Mrs. Dunny?" I said, turning to the camera. The audience laughed. "Everybody else has to do it the hard way and here you are reading it from my mind. Let's see how you do on the questions. Are you ready?"

She nodded.

"Name the one and only mammal that has the ability to fly," I asked.

"A bat," she said.

"Right! Did you read that from my mind?"

"Oh, yes, you're coming over very clear!" said Mrs. Dunny.

"How about this one? Is a Kodiak a kind of simple box camera; a type of double-bowed boat; or a type of Alaskan bear?"

"A bear," said Mrs. Dunny.

"Very good," I said. "That was a hard one." I asked her seven more questions and she got them all right. I wound up giving her the gas range and other smaller prizes.

After we were off the air I followed the audience out into the hall. Mrs. Dunny was walking towards the lobby with an old paper shopping bag under her arm. An attendant was following her with an armful of prizes.

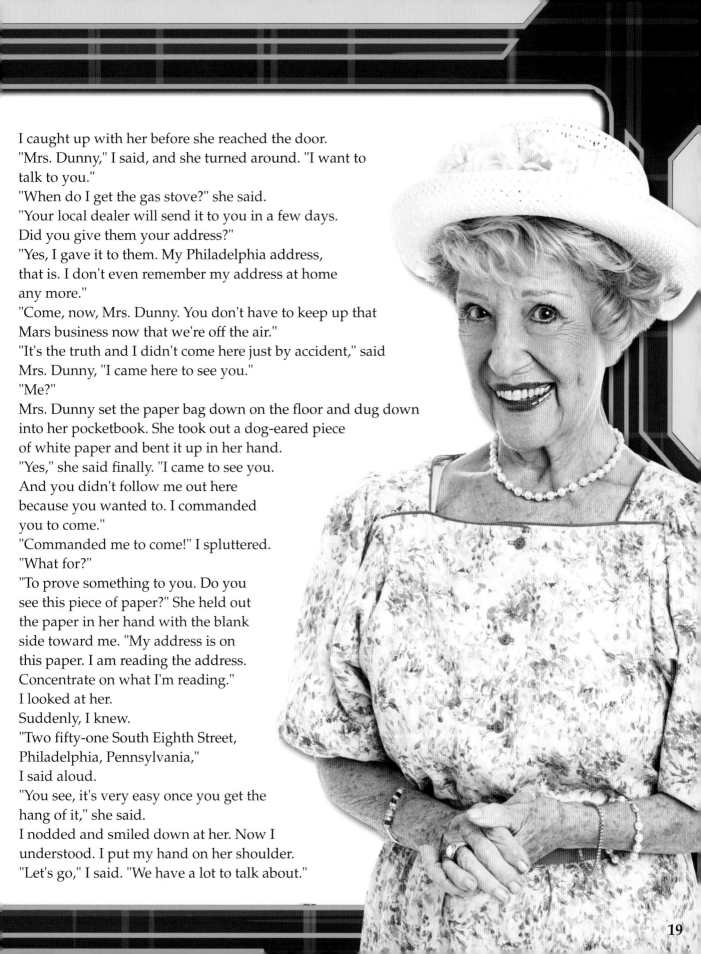

I caught up with her before she reached the door.
"Mrs. Dunny," I said, and she turned around. "I want to talk to you."
"When do I get the gas stove?" she said.
"Your local dealer will send it to you in a few days. Did you give them your address?"
"Yes, I gave it to them. My Philadelphia address, that is. I don't even remember my address at home any more."
"Come, now, Mrs. Dunny. You don't have to keep up that Mars business now that we're off the air."
"It's the truth and I didn't come here just by accident," said Mrs. Dunny, "I came here to see you."
"Me?"
Mrs. Dunny set the paper bag down on the floor and dug down into her pocketbook. She took out a dog-eared piece of white paper and bent it up in her hand.
"Yes," she said finally. "I came to see you. And you didn't follow me out here because you wanted to. I commanded you to come."
"Commanded me to come!" I spluttered. "What for?"
"To prove something to you. Do you see this piece of paper?" She held out the paper in her hand with the blank side toward me. "My address is on this paper. I am reading the address. Concentrate on what I'm reading."
I looked at her.
Suddenly, I knew.
"Two fifty-one South Eighth Street, Philadelphia, Pennsylvania,"
I said aloud.
"You see, it's very easy once you get the hang of it," she said.
I nodded and smiled down at her. Now I understood. I put my hand on her shoulder.
"Let's go," I said. "We have a lot to talk about."

ALIENS AND OTHER CHARACTERS

There are only two characters in the science fiction story *One Out of Ten*.

The main character is the game show host. He is a nice man who smiles a lot.

The second character tells us more about the host. Mrs. Freda Dunny is the game show contestant. She is honest and straightforward. She also has special powers. Mrs. Dunny can read minds. We also know that Mrs. Dunny is not human. She is a Martian.

WHAT IF...?

Ideas for great science fiction stories often start with the phrase "what if..." What if there was another universe? What if we could travel in far outer space? What if the Martian characters from *One Out of Ten* met the robots from *The Helpful Robots*? How would these characters react to one another? Do you think they would get along? Why or why not? Write down your answers.

Characters can face problems that come out nowhere. Or the problem may result from something they have done.

The talk show host is a nice guy. Rod Rankin in *The Helpful Robots* is not. They both have a problem to face.

The talk show host faces a problem not of his own making.

Rod Rankin's own actions caused his problem.

DIALOGUE: KEEPING IT REAL

Dialogue is conversation between characters in a story.

It is a useful tool for building worlds and developing characters. In *One Out of Ten*, nobody takes Mrs. Dunny very seriously. Her dialogue is direct, but lighthearted to start. The dialogue gets serious when her character needs to get down to business. The game show host starts out happy and smiling. He becomes unsure of himself for a moment, then finds himself again.

Look for this in the following piece of dialogue:

"Yes," she said finally. "I came to see you. And you didn't follow me out here because you wanted to. I commanded you to come."

"Commanded me to come!" I spluttered. "What for?"

"To prove something to you. Do you see this piece of paper?" She held out the paper in her hand with the blank side toward me. "My address is on this paper. I am reading the address. Concentrate on what I'm reading."

I looked at her.

Suddenly, I knew.

 ## WAYS TO SAY "SAID"

How many different ways are there for a writer to show who is speaking? He said. She said. I said. In *One Out of Ten*, the game show host splutters. Brainstorm a list of other words a writer can use to show who is speaking.

SETTING:
AN UNREAL REALITY

Many science fiction stories are set in the future. Some are set in space, on different worlds or even different universes. *One Out of Ten* is set on Earth in a familiar setting. There is no need for the writer to spend a lot of time describing a setting which readers already know about.

How does the setting of *One Out of Ten* differ from the setting of *The Helpful Robots*? What words are used to help set the different settings? How would the setting of *One Out of Ten* be different if the game show was set on Mars instead of Earth?

BUILDING THE SCENE

How would you describe the setting of the game show to someone who has never been to Earth before? How big is it? What shape? How many rooms? How long is the hallway leading to the door where Mrs. Dunny and the game show host have their final conversation? Write down your answers. Use these answers to build a cardboard version of what the game show building looks like.

SCIENCE FICTION PLOTS: MAPPING THE STORY

In *One Out of Ten*, a game show host introduces a guest who claims to be from Mars. The guest reads the host's mind and wins all the prizes. Her real reason for being there is to let the game show host know that he is a Martian as well.

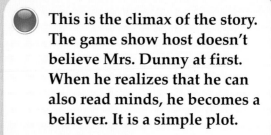

This is the climax of the story. The game show host doesn't believe Mrs. Dunny at first. When he realizes that he can also read minds, he becomes a believer. It is a simple plot.

STORY MAP FOR *ONE OUT OF TEN*

Characters

● Game Show Host, Mrs. Freda Dunny

Settings

● Game show stage, hallway

Problem

● The game show host is a Martian, but he does not know this fact.

Events

1. Game show host introduces Mrs. Dunny.

2. Mrs. Dunny says she is from Mars and can read minds.

3. Mrs. Dunny answers all the questions and wins all the prizes.

4. The game show host reads Mrs. Dunny's mind.

5. Climax: The game show host realizes he is a Martian.

Resolution

● He wants to talk to Mrs. Dunny to learn more about what comes next.

Lesson

● Things are not always as they appear to be.

THEME: WHAT IS IT ABOUT?

Themes in science fiction can open our eyes about the future of our society and our world. The future in science fiction is not always pretty. It can include disasters or the breakdown of society due to greed or war.

One Out of Ten was written in 1956, not long after World War II. Astronaut Neil Armstrong had not yet walked on the moon. At the time, people were questioning whether there was life outside of our own planet. Alien life was a common theme in science fiction stories.

COMPARE AND CONTRAST

Comparing and contrasting are ways to look at things. When you compare two things, you are looking at how they are the same. When you contrast two things, you are looking at how they are different.

Write a few paragraphs comparing and contrasting the theme of *One Out of Ten* with the theme of *The Helpful Robots*. How are they similar? How are they different?

CREATIVE RESPONSE TO THE SCIENCE FICTION STORY

ALIEN ART

Draw a picture of what you think an alien would look like. Below the picture, write a brief description of your alien's strange features.

GET CREATIVE

Create a game. Build an alien staircase out of cardboard. It must be at least 15 steps. Place a paper mat labeled "On your mark" at the bottom. On each step, write down a positive or negative event. (For example, "Starship blown up by earthmen and you must return to 'On your mark.'" OR "Avoid battle with aliens and move ahead two steps.") Build alien figures out of modeling clay. Roll dice. Highest goes first. Roll again and climb that number of steps. Follow instructions on the step you land on. Now it is the next person's turn. The goal is to be the first to get to the top step.

WRITE A LETTER

Pretend you are writing a letter to the author of *One Out of Ten*. Ask him why he chose to write this story. Include at least two other questions you might have about this work of science fiction.

Introduction: Getting the Audience's Attention

At the beginning of every LD case is an introduction. Like a persuasive speech, the introduction starts with an attention-getting device to introduce the audience to the topic and interest them in what the debater is going to say. This device is often a persuasive quotation or statistic that relates to the case. It should come from an author who has experience in the subject of the debate and should be easy for the audience to understand. After the attention-getter, the debater shifts to the resolution with a brief explanation of what the quotation or statistic means and how it either helps support the resolution or prove it wrong. Next, the debater clearly states the resolution as it is written. Here's an example of an introduction to a case:

Voter turnout and other areas of citizen participation in our nation's affairs continue to decline. Yet at the same time, crises in other nations shed light on the fact that many of us take our good fortune for granted. Continuing conflict in China, Cuba, and Guatemala illustrates the dangers of oppressive government. Chaos in Somalia, Sierra Leone, and the former Yugoslavia demonstrates the problems of anarchy. Former secretary of state Henry Kissinger once said, "Seldom are we faced with a decision between right and wrong . . . more often than not, we must determine the least harmful course of action." Today, we face a similar problem. As a result, I will prove that even an oppressive government is better than no government.

You can see that the introduction starts with a description of problems in other countries around the world, includes a quote from a famous former statesman, then states the resolution and what side of the argument the debater will support.

Defining Your Resolution

The next part of the introduction is the definition of important words and phrases in the resolution. Definitions are important because people have different understandings of the same words. It's important to make sure the audience knows what the words mean in the context of the resolution. When defining words, debaters need to define whole phrases when possible, instead of individual words. For example, instead of defining both "political" and "oppression," debaters should define the phrase "political oppression." Also, debaters should define only words that are most likely to need to be defined. It is more important to define "eminent domain," for instance, than "government." Not everyone knows what eminent domain is, but most people know what government is.

There are many places to find good definitions. The best way to determine what words mean is by reading as much as possible about the topic to find out what the experts say. Definitions determined this way are called contextual definitions. Contextual definitions describe the concepts in the

Black's Law Dictionary

resolution as they are commonly used, or any special meaning they have in relation to the subject of the resolution.

Another good place to look for definitions is in a well-respected dictionary. *Black's Law Dictionary* is a legal dictionary that defines words and concepts the way they are used in the American legal system. It is helpful for legal words and phrases such as "rights," "eminent domain," and "social welfare." Other common dictionaries are helpful, too, but debaters need to be careful which definitions they choose for their cases. Sometimes a word's dictionary definition doesn't mean what the resolution intends the word to mean. The most important thing to remember when trying to find definitions is to stay true to what the resolution means. This is what a debater might say to lead into the definitions:

For clarity in today's debate, I offer the following definitions taken from *Black's Law Dictionary*:

oppressive government A government that, through its institutions, withholds from the people internationally recognized civil, economic, and/or human rights.

no government A nation-state existing without formal institutions that provide control and benefits to its citizens.

Since both definitions come from the same place, the debater introduces them by telling us what source they are from. Also, notice that terms are defined, not individual words. "Oppressive government" is defined as a single term, not as separate words.

The Value Premise

After the definitions come the value premise and the criterion. These two components are what make LD debate different from other types of debate. The value premise is a social value that is highlighted within the context of the resolution. For example, many people think concepts such as freedom, identity (who we are), and individualism (being ourselves separate from society) are very important to our society.

If the resolution is "An oppressive government is better than no government," debaters should consider what people would find important whether they're in support of the resolution or not. Something that is valuable in society is stability, which keeps things in order and keeps us safe. It doesn't matter which side of the resolution the debater is on—stability is important both to a society that thinks an oppressive government is better than no government and to a society that thinks no government at all is better. Debaters will want to find a value that will be applicable regardless of the resolution.

As part of the introduction, the debater should state the value (the most important goal) and give a definition so everyone understands what it is and why it's important. The debater should also explain how the value they chose relates to the resolution overall. This is what a value paragraph might look like:

> The affirmative will uphold the value of self-actualization. Self-actualization means the individual has ample opportunity to determine for himself or herself what is necessary for a happy life. Self-actualization is important for the resolution because the system of government (or lack thereof) should be determined more or less valuable based on the quality of space the individual has for this self-actualization.

Notice that the value is stated, then defined. Then there is a short explanation of what it means and how it relates to the resolution. In this case, self-actualization relates to the resolution because any situation is said to be good or bad based on the amount of freedom a person has to decide things for himself or herself.

Choosing the Criterion

Next, the debater will choose a criterion to help support their value. A criterion can have different purposes. It can show how the debater plans to achieve their value premise. For example, a value of stability may require individual choice in some societies. When people are involved in decisions and can make their own choices, they are more likely to be happy. Regarding the resolution "An oppressive government is better than no government," the negative might say stability is best achieved when all individuals in society feel their ability to choose is being respected. The negative would then use their arguments to show how not having a government would best lead to people having choice, which would support the value of stability. An example of the affirmative criterion might be:

In order to determine which position in today's round best provides opportunity for self-actualization, the affirmative proposes the criterion of participation. This means that the individual has the best opportunity to interact with society regardless of the type of governing system in place. This criterion is important to the value of self-actualization because without the ability to interact meaningfully with society, the individual will be unable to determine for himself or herself what is beneficial and what isn't.

15

By using the criterion to achieve the value, this debater starts by saying what participation is and why it's important to self-actualization. Arguments about how the affirmative will achieve participation and self-actualization are saved for the main part of the case. Here, all the debater does is set up the most important goal and how it will be accomplished.

Another less common way the criterion can be used is as a definition for the value. If the value is broad and could have several different definitions, the criterion would then help clarify what the value actually means. For example, the value of justice would require a pretty long explanation, since justice is a general concept that can mean many things. The criterion in this case would be what the debater has decided justice really means. In this case, the criterion might be "giving each person what he or she deserves." Regardless of what criterion is chosen, the debater needs to define the concept with a contextual or dictionary definition and explain why this criterion is necessary to achieve the value.

The Thesis

The final part of the introduction is the thesis. A thesis is a statement of the overall argument the debater plans to make in the rest of their case. A thesis generally begins with a statement of the resolution (including what side the debater is on) and the relationship of the value and criterion to that side of the resolution. A sample thesis could look like this:

> An oppressive government is better than no government because oppressive government will make social interaction more possible than an absence of government, and that will lead to better self-actualization for the individual.

This thesis statement begins with the resolution, then relates the value and criterion to the topic. This will be the main argument the debater will be trying to prove with different supporting arguments.

The Body of the Case

The body of the case is where the debater presents their main arguments. A debater should have two or three main points. If a debater has more than that, the main points are probably not explained well enough. If a debater has fewer than that, then the only main point they have is probably too complex and will require too much explanation. Each main argument is called a contention. A contention will begin with a tagline, which is a simple sentence that states what the argument will be. After the tagline, the debater will explain their major argument. This is what the case might look like when it's put together:

Introduction and Resolution Analysis	Voter turnout and other areas of citizen participation in our nation's affairs continue to decline. Yet at the same time, crises in other nations shed light on the fact that many of us take our good fortune for granted. Continuing conflict in China, Cuba, and Guatemala illustrates the dangers of oppressive government. Chaos in Somalia, Sierra Leone, and the former Yugoslavia demonstrates the problems of anarchy. Former secretary of state Henry Kissinger once noted, "Seldom are we faced with a decision between right and wrong . . . more often than not, we must determine the least harmful course of action." As a result, I stand in affirmation that an oppressive government is better than no government.

Definitions	For clarity in today's debate, I offer the following definitions taken from *Black's Law Dictionary:*
	oppressive government A government that, through its institutions, withholds from the people internationally recognized civil, economic, and/or human rights.
	no government A nation-state existing without formal institutions that provide control and benefits to its citizens.
Value Premise	The affirmative will uphold the value of self-actualization. Self-actualization means the individual has ample opportunity to determine for himself or herself what is necessary for a happy life. Self-actualization is important for the resolution because the system of government (or lack thereof) should be determined more or less valuable based on the quality of space the individual has for this self-actualization.

WRITING A SCIENCE FICTION STORY

You've learned all about characters, dialogue, settings, and plots. Now write your own science fiction short story.

1 **Ready, Set, Don't Start Yet**
Write a list of ideas for your science fiction story. Choose a subject. Gather ideas for characters, plot, theme, and setting. Organize your ideas.

2 **Drive Those Characters**
Choose one main character. Give that character one main trait. Are they proud, smart, forgetful, or sloppy? Does this trait get the character into trouble?

3 **Problems?**
Take your main character and give them a problem. Write a sentence that tells about the character and their problem.

Sarah is abducted by aliens and she is going to be late for lunch. She has low blood sugar and this could turn into a serious matter if she doesn't act quickly!

Joey flies a kite that pulls him into a fantasy world in the future and he must find his way back to Earth. His problem is he keeps getting distracted!

Lexi gets carsick just thinking about getting into the car. How is she going to handle a trip to Planet Zenock in a time machine?

Map It Out

Make a **story map** for the science fiction story you would like to write. Be sure to include the main events. Who will be introduced? What will happen at the beginning of the story? What kind of problem will the main character face in the middle? What events solve the problem? How does the story end?

First Draft

Use your notes from prewriting. Get your ideas down on paper. Do not worry about mistakes. This is just the first draft. Let your creative energy flow!

The aliens had Colby cornered. He couldn't resist. They raised their arms and suddenly he was lying flat on his back. His body was above the floor. It was like he was lying on his bed.

He watched as one alien held up one finger. Colby's cast disappeared. Another alien shut his eyes. Colby's arm stretched like an elastic band until it reached the far side of the room. It did not hurt. The tall alien snapped his fingers. Colby's arm snapped back into place. He held up a finger, shut his eyes and his arm stretched to the far side of the room. Wow Colby thought to himself that's a cool trick. That's the last he remembered before he fell back to sleep.

Waking up for school, Colby thought about the strange dream he had the night before.. No way that could be real. He reached down to pull the covers off. That's when he noticed it. His cast was gone. He shut his eyes and imagined his arm reaching across the room. When he opened his eyes, there were socks were dangling in his hand. Boy, he thought as he raced out the door, was he ever going to be popular today!

6 Revise, Revise, Revise!

Read your draft a couple of times. Does it make sense? Decide what changes need to be made. Add a few more details to boost interest. Polish the ending.

The three aliens had Colby cornered. He couldn't resist the pull of their gaze. They raised their arms and suddenly he was lying flat on his back. His body floated above the floor. It was like he was lying on his bed, only there was no bed.

He watched as the blue alien held up one finger. Colby's cast disappeared. The alien with six eyes shut two of his eyes. Colby's arm stretched like an elastic band until it reached the far side of the room. Strange, but it did not hurt. The tall, skinny alien with four hands snapped his fingers. Colby's arm snapped back into place. He held up a finger, shut his eyes and his arm stretched to the far side of the room. Wow! Colby thought to himself, that's a cool trick. That's the last he remembered before he fell back to sleep.

Waking up for school, Colby thought about the strange dream he had the night before. Weird, he thought. No way that could be real. He reached down to pull the covers off. That's when he noticed it. His cast was gone. He shut his eyes and imagined his arm reaching across the room to grab clean socks from the sock drawer. When he opened his eyes, the socks were dangling in his hand. Boy, he thought as he raced out of the bedroom door, was he ever going to be popular at school today!

The Proof Is in the Reading
When you edit and proofread, make sure your writing is clear and accurate.

- Check your spelling.
- Fix punctuation mistakes.
- Fix capitalization mistakes.
- Fix other grammar mistakes.

Spotlight, Please!
Write up a clean copy of your science fiction story. Give it a title. Add a few pictures to help show what is happening in your story. Share the final copy with your family and friends.

Congratulations, Earthling! You have just written a science fiction story!

GLOSSARY

Please note: Some bold-faced words are defined in the text

character	The person or things that are speaking in the story
conflict	A problem that the main character has to solve; a problem that causes trouble
cylindrical	Shaped like a cylinder, or a wide roll
dialogue	The words a character speaks
drama	A story that is performed as a play on a stage
fantasy	A story that could not happen in the real world
jurisdiction	The territory in which a particular system of laws is used
plantation	A large area of land where crops are grown
poem	Short groups of words that tell a story
prose	A story written in sentences and paragraphs
resolution	The end of the story, when the plot's main problem is solved
setting	The place where and time when the story takes place
science fiction	A story that uses both fantasy and science
story map	A diagram that shows the basic parts of the plot
verandah	A porch that has a roof over it

INDEX

FURTHER RESOURCES

Books:

Captain Underpants and the Revolting Revenge of the Radioactive Robo-Boxers by Dav Pilkey. Scholastic Inc. (2013)

Franny K. Stein Mad Scientist: Lunch Walks Among Us by Jim Benton. Scholastic Inc. (2004)

The Transmogrification of Roscoe Wizzle by Dave Elliott. Candlewick. (2001)

Zita the Spacegirl by Ben Hatke. First Second. (2011)

Websites:

Design a Martian (with NASA)
http://quest.nasa.gov/projects/astrobiology/astroventure/challenge/index.html

Questions to Consider While Reading Science Fiction
www.readwritethink.org/files/resources/lesson_images/lesson927/SciFiQuestions.pdf

Science Fiction Story Starters
www.scholastic.com/teachers/story-starters/science-fiction-writing-prompts/